THE LAST WORDS
OF CHRIST ON THE CROSS

"Not in bread alone doth man live, but in every word that proceedeth from the mouth of God." —Matthew 4:4

THE SEVEN
LAST WORDS
OF CHRIST ON THE CROSS

Fr. Christopher Rengers, O.F.M. Cap.

*"Heaven and earth shall pass away,
but my words shall not pass away."*
—Luke 21:33

TAN BOOKS AND PUBLISHERS, INC.
Rockford, Illinois 61105

Imprimi Potest: Very Rev. Claude Vogel, O.F.M. Cap.
                           Minister Provincial
                           October 7, 1957

Nihil Obstat: John A. Schulien, S.T.D.
                           Censor Librorum

Imprimatur: ✠ Albert G. Meyer
                           Archbishop of Milwaukee
                           November 22, 1957

Retypeset and republished in 2002 by TAN Books and Publishers, Inc. under the title *The Seven Last Words*.

ISBN 0-89555-731-2

Cover illustration of the Crucifixion: painting by Janssens from his series of seven illustrations of the Seven Sorrows of Mary, distributed by the Servite Fathers, Chicago.

Printed and bound in the United States of America.

TAN BOOKS AND PUBLISHERS, INC.
P.O. Box 424
Rockford, Illinois 61105
2002

"Thou hast the words of eternal life."
—*John* 6:69

CONTENTS

THE SEVEN LAST WORDS

OF CHRIST ON THE CROSS

"The words that I have spoken to you are spirit and life." —John 6:64

"Father, forgive them, for they know
not what they do."   —*Luke* 23:34

Forgiveness

THE first words that Jesus spoke after being
nailed to the Cross were words of forgiveness. He had gone through much suffering
and strain. He had been taken from court to
court, from Caiphas to Pilate to Herod and back to
Pilate. He had felt the angry tide of human passion explode against Him in false testimony, in
insults and in shouting for His death. He had
already sweat blood, had been scourged and
crowned with thorns. He had walked the exhausting, bitter steps carrying His Cross to Calvary
and had been stripped of His garments.

He Forgives

But no doubt the actual nailing to the Cross
brings with it a new and more severe pain. The
long, roughly shaped spikes tearing through His
hands and feet not only burn like fire but send
new throbs of pain throughout His whole body.
Most of the poor slaves or criminals who were

1

executed by crucifixion screamed and shouted in despair at this point. Ordinarily all this new, intense suffering wrung words from the mouth of the victim of crucifixion. But Christ put into practice what He had counseled, by praying for those who were His enemies. The height of physical pain wrung from His lips only the words of forgiveness: "Father, forgive them." He asked forgiveness for the soldiers, for the Jews who had maneuvered His execution, for all who by sinning in the years to come were to co-operate in His death.

He Excuses

Christ added words of excuse: "For they know not what they do." No doubt these words applied most fully to the Roman soldiers, for they were just the rough instruments of execution. But the words were put forth as a plea for all, considering the blindness of human reason and the force of passion on the human will. The high priests and other leaders knew quite well what they were doing, but even for them the enormity of the crime may not have been altogether clear. Our Lord prayed for their forgiveness.

He had much to forgive even as a man, abstracting from the fact of His Divine Nature. These people who had brought on Him so much pain and disgrace were the very ones whom He had been trying to help. He had spent the past few years going about their country preaching, working miracles, even raising the dead from the grave. Yet, they closed their eyes to all this. They invented lies, tried to make it appear that this Man who lived in poverty, who had fled when some would make Him king, was plotting to overthrow the government and take over the power for Himself and His followers. The accusations against Him during the trial were absolutely false, as Pontius Pilate, the neutral Roman, also recognized.

Hard to Take

Most of us probably know from experience that if there is anything hard to take, it is a deliberately false accusation. If we are accused of something we have not done, our blood begins to boil immediately, and angry words rush to our lips. When false accusations come from ones we have been trying to help, they are even harder to take, for the ingratitude stings us. Yet this is exactly the situation, humanly speaking, that Christ found Himself in. To false accusation, to ingrained ingratitude, He reacts by a prayer for forgiveness.

St. Stephen

St. Stephen, the first martyr, comes to mind as a striking instance of one who followed the example of his Master in forgiving. His words of wisdom and truth so cut the Jewish leaders to the heart that they gnashed their teeth. They took

Stephen out and cast stones at him. But while they were stoning him to death, he fell on his knees and prayed: "Lord, lay not this sin to their charge." (*Acts* 7:59). He could have called out to those who stoned him: "Do not forget that there is a just God, and that you will be punished for this!" Filled with the spirit of Christ, he prayed for the forgiveness of his enemies.

So have the true followers of Christ acted through the ages. The lives of Saints are full of examples of ready forgiveness. The early martyrs prayed for their executioners. From our own shores have come stories of those who were tortured, yet prayed for those who tortured them.

In March of 1649, Father Jean de Brébeuf endured martyrdom at the hands of the Iroquois Indians. Many times he spoke the words: "Jesus, have mercy on us," begging perseverance for himself and the other Christian prisoners, and forgiveness for their tormentors. The Indians poured scalding water over his head, jesting that without this baptism he could not be saved. "Jesus, have mercy on us" was his answer. He asked that God might forgive them since they did not know what they were doing, and would lead them all to a true Baptism. In fury at not being able to break Father de Brébeuf's spirit, the Iroquois cut off his nose and upper lip. Unable to endure his prayers for mercy for them, they cut out his tongue. Even

Note: St. John de Brébeuf was responsible for the conversion of some 7,000 souls. —*Publisher,* 2002.

then, the dying martyr forced from his tongueless mouth a hoarse, guttural: "Jesus, have mercy!"

St. John Gualbert

Back in the eleventh century, a man by the name of John Gualbert set out to avenge the death of his brother, Hugh. Hugh had been murdered, and John swore that he would kill the murderer. The father, also full of sorrow and resentment, encouraged him. John was a soldier and considered it upholding his honor to make up for the death of an only brother. So he set out to look for the killer.

He met him on Good Friday in a passage so narrow that there was no escape. The man was unarmed and fell on his knees. He stretched out his arms in the form of a cross and asked, for the love of Jesus Crucified, to be forgiven his crime. John Gualbert did not hesitate long. He responded to grace and forgave the man in the name of Jesus Crucified; he even went forward and embraced him. God did not allow John to go unrewarded, but filled his soul with grace, leading him to the monastery, where he was to lead a strict and holy life. The Catholic Church now celebrates the Feast of St. John Gualbert on July 12. Had he refused the plea for forgiveness, he would himself have become a vindictive murderer. But he forgave and became a Saint.

Forgiveness a Duty

To forgive is a duty. In the sermon on the Mount Our Lord said: "You have heard that it hath been said, Thou shalt love thy neighbour, and hate thy enemy. But I say to you, Love your enemies: do good to them that hate you: and pray for them that persecute and calumniate you: that you may be the children of your Father who is in Heaven, who maketh his sun to rise upon the good, and bad, and raineth upon the just and the unjust." (*Matt.* 5:43-45). He then went on to say that even the heathens saluted and loved those who were friendly to them; that was only natural. What reward could you expect for being friendly to those who were good to you? The commandment of Our Lord was not a commandment merely to be friendly to other people in general. It was a specific command to love and do good to those who have done evil to us.

Not Always Easy

This does not mean to say that to forgive is always easy to do. In certain cases it may take great effort to forgive. Suppose somebody causes you to lose a good job; imagine somebody who deliberately ruined your health; put yourself in the position of St. John Gualbert, whose brother was murdered. No matter what effort it takes, no matter how greatly we have been wronged, the commandment of Christ stands. We must forgive.

"I say to you, love your enemies."

In some instances the wrong we suffer is genuine. In many more instances, it is much more a matter of hurt feelings and often of childishness that creates the wrongs. Very often the whole case can be seen by an unprejudiced observer to be a matter of pride. Perhaps there were some words spoken to us in anger, not altogether justifiable. The person who spoke them may regret his words very soon. But we rear up in indignation and make a big thing of them. Long after our "enemy" has humbly accused himself in Confession of harsh words, they still rankle in our hearts. A long-term grudge begins. There is not really much to forgive; but by refusing to forgive, the grudge becomes solidified. As time goes on, it is usually harder to forgive.

Refusal Hurts Oneself

To refuse to forgive does not in most cases harm the other person; but in all cases it harms the one who refuses to forgive. First of all, the person who refuses forgiveness harms his own soul by the sin of refusal, by going against the *express command* of Christ. Sometimes he plunges his soul into still further sin by cutting himself off from some good work in which he was engaged, for example, from some parish society that the other person also attends. The saddest cases are those who cut themselves off from the Church and the Sacraments. For some real or imagined wrong committed against them by a priest or some representative of the Church, such a person stops going to church.

More than 70 years ago a young man was told by a priest to take the family pew near the front of the church. He preferred to remain in the rear. When the priest insisted, the young man walked out of church. He never returned, for he could not forgive that order given to him before the congregation. The young man grew up, then married outside of the Church. His children grew up without the benefits of the truth and the Sacraments of the Church established by Jesus Christ. So did his grandchildren. The young man, grown old, died not long ago. More than 60 of his descendants live on, not one of them a child of the Church. Had this man forgiven, instead of having all this to answer for, perhaps he might have children or grandchildren in the convent or priesthood. Refusal to forgive harms the soul, and often the damage passes on to many other souls.

To refuse to forgive may also damage the mind and even the body. For it creates bitterness of spirit and blinds the mind to many of the good and happy things of creation. The effects of bitterness of mind can overflow into the body and bring on or increase physical disease.

On the contrary, to forgive may actually shame your enemy, supposing real wrong to have been done, and bring him to repentance. St. Paul says: "If thy enemy be hungry, give him to eat; if he thirst, give him to drink. For, doing this, thou shalt heap coals of fire upon his head." (*Rom.* 12:20).

Brings New Graces

Forgiveness sets the stage for receiving new graces; lack of forgiveness blocks grace. Nowhere is this more true than in the reception of Holy Communion. To receive the full benefits of this Sacrament of love, we must be at peace with all men. Our Lord said: "If therefore thou offer thy gift at the altar, and there thou remember that thy brother hath any thing against thee; leave there thy offering before the altar, and go first to be reconciled to thy brother: and then coming thou shalt offer thy gift." (*Matt.* 5:23-24). This was said originally to those who came to offer gifts of sacrifice according to the Old Law. It applies even more so to those who offer the Eternal Sacrifice of the Mass in the New Law, and who participate in the sacrifice through Holy Communion. It is a good practice in preparing for Holy Communion to forgive from the heart all who may have done anything that requires forgiveness. Only then are we fit to participate fully in the union of our souls with Christ who forgave His enemies even in the midst of His greatest pain.

No Limit

St. Peter asked one day, when Christ had been talking on the subject of brotherly love: "Lord, how often shall my brother offend against me, and I forgive him? Till seven times?" Peter thought he was being very generous in setting a high number. But the answer was: "I say not to thee, till seven times; but till seventy times seven times." (*Matt.* 18:21-22). In short, there is no limit to the forgiveness that is demanded of us. God will always take care of just punishment. It is up to us to forgive.

Forgive Us . . . As We Forgive

Each day as we pray the Our Father, the prayer taught to us by His eternal Son, we pray to be forgiven even as we forgive—"Forgive us our trespasses, as we forgive those who trespass against us." If we do not forgive those who trespass against us, we are actually praying to God *not* to forgive us our own sins. We pray to be forgiven as we forgive.

Robert Louis Stevenson, the English author, the writer of *Treasure Island* and other stories, was one night leading the prayers in his family circle. When he came to the words: "Forgive us our trespasses," he jumped up and went outside. After about twenty minutes he returned and, with great emotion, finished the prayers. Later he explained to his wife and children: "When I came to those words, 'Forgive as I wish to forgive others,' I thought of a certain man who had offended me today. Feelings of hatred stirred up in my heart. I could not go on with that beautiful prayer until I had fought these feelings down and made

myself forgive as I asked to be forgiven." During
the time that Robert Louis Stevenson was gone,
he had conquered his feelings and gone to the
home of the offender and assured him that all was
well between them.

All of us hope that God will forgive us our sins.
All of us have sinned, and perhaps mortally, many
times. If we expect forgiveness, we must extend it
to others. Otherwise, we will be like the unmerci-
ful servant spoken of by Our Lord. (*Matt.* 18:23-
35). This man was called by the king to pay a very
large debt. But he had no means of paying, so the
king ordered him to be sold, together with his wife
and children. But the servant fell down and
besought the king, saying: "Have patience with
me, and I will pay thee all." So the king, moved by
compassion, released him and canceled the entire
debt. Then this servant, going out, met a fellow
servant who owed him a small debt. He laid hold
of him and demanded payment. The fellow servant fell down before him, saying: "Have patience
with me, and I will pay thee all." But the first servant would not listen, and instead had him cast
into prison. When the king was informed of this,
he called in the first servant and said to him:
"Wicked servant, I forgave thee all the debt,
because thou besoughtest me: shouldst not thou
then have had compassion also on thy fellow servant, even as I had compassion on thee?" And
being angry, he handed him over to the torturers
until he should pay all. At the end of this parable,
Our Lord said: "So also shall my heavenly Father

do to you, if you forgive not every one his brother from your hearts."

Any time that we feel resentment and the growing of hard feelings and grudges within us, let us remember these things. Above all, let us look back to Calvary and remember the words of Our Lord: "Father, forgive them, for they know not what they do."

∽ SECOND WORD ∽

"Amen I say to thee, this day thou shalt be with me in paradise."

—*Luke* 23:43

The Mercy of God to Sinners

WHEN a man is in great pain or dying, even his worst enemies will ordinarily leave him in peace. It would be unthinkable to walk into the sickroom of a dying man and make fun of him and taunt him. Such things are done only when savagery and the passion of hate are given full sway. Such things have happened under the banner of Communism, which denies God and which strips man of worth and dignity. This materialistic philosophy makes man an animal, so it may treat him like an animal or worse. Such things also happened while Christ was hanging on the Cross. His enemies derided Him, scoffed at Him and mocked Him while He hung dying in pain.

Cruel Fun

Our Lord had at one time said that when "this temple" would be torn down, He would rebuild it

13

in three days. He referred to the temple of His body, meaning that He would rise again. Walking by the Cross, His enemies taunted Him with this: "Vah, thou that destroyest the temple of God, and in three days buildest it up again; save thyself, coming down from the cross." (*Mark* 15:29-30).

Even Our Lord's miracles were held up to scorn: "He saved others; himself he cannot save. Let Christ the king of Israel come down now from the cross, that we may see and believe." (*Mark* 15:31-32). Also, Our Lord's trust in God was held up to blasphemous ridicule. "He trusted in God; let him now deliver *him* if he will have him; for he said: I am the Son of God." (*Matt.* 27:43). The soldiers at first spent some time in casting lots for Christ's seamless garment. Later they joined in the cruel fun, coming up to the Cross and saying: "If thou be the king of the Jews, save thyself." (*Luke* 23:37). One of the thieves also blasphemed Him, saying, "If thou be Christ, save thyself and us." (*Luke* 23:39).

A Guarantee

To all this, which no doubt went on for some time, Christ replied not a single word. Yet He replied immediately to what was said by the thief crucified at His right. This man rebuked the thief on the left hand for his blasphemy. He told him that he should fear God, since he was soon about to die. "And we indeed justly," he continued, "for we receive the due reward of our deeds; but this man hath done no evil." (*Luke* 23:41). Then he said to Jesus: "Lord, remember me when thou shalt come into thy kingdom." The answer was a promise and a reassurance that went far beyond the request: "Amen I say to thee, this day thou shalt be with me in paradise." (*Luke* 23:43).

The thief had diffidently asked merely to be remembered. He was given a guarantee of saving his soul and of eternal happiness.

He Stole Heaven

The *Roman Martyrology,* which is the book listing all the saints, lists under March 25: "the Good Thief." Those two words, which you would not expect to find together, are the words that have come down to describe the man at the right of Christ. We do not really know his name, though the name St. Dismas is used most often in referring to him. Of this man, St. Augustine said with both wisdom and wit that he remained a thief to the very end, such that after being a thief all his life, he finally ended by stealing Heaven.

If we examine the words of this man and their meaning, we find that in a simple way he really went to Confession while hanging on his cross. Christ, the great Priest, in the very act of accomplishing His sacrifice, absolved him and, so to speak, granted him a plenary indulgence.

In the course of time various legends grew up around the Good Thief, but all we actually know about him is contained in the few lines of the

Gospel of St. Luke. Still, even in these few lines there is a good bit of information. Dismas did something that even most of the followers and friends of Christ did not do. He supported Him and called Him *Lord* in the midst of His enemies. We might say: "Well, he didn't have anything to lose; he was already on the cross, soon to die." But it takes courage at all times to go against the crowd, especially when the crowd includes religious leaders of a people, and especially when it is so wrought up with passions as was the crowd on Calvary.

Admits Sins

The Good Thief confessed his guilt and admitted that he was just paying the penalty that he deserved. He had the humility and the honesty to admit his sins and to accept this terrible punishment of crucifixion. Finally, he had faith. To us today it may not seem much to have called Christ on the Cross, "Lord," and to have asked for remembrance in His kingdom. Yet it took great faith to see God in the broken, suffering Man on the next cross, apparently the victim of the schemes of His enemies. To call Christ "Lord," after He had just worked a miracle was one thing; to call Him "Lord," now was altogether different. Even the Apostles could hardly accept the frightening fact of their Master's apparent inability to outwit and to foil the plans of those who sought His life, and hence His hanging twisted and bloody in the agony and disgrace of a criminal's death.

The Good Thief had sorrow for his sins; he confessed his guilt; he had faith; and finally he had hope; otherwise, he could not have asked for a place in the world to come. The Good Thief had the right dispositions for forgiveness. Therefore, despite his life of sin against God and man, he was forgiven and promised Heaven.

Readiness of Mercy

The mercy of God is always ready to reach out to and save a soul, even at the last minute, if only that soul co-operates, if there is humble admission of guilt, if there is still faith and hope. It does not take long—just a minute—to get right again with God, even after a lifetime of sin.

Of course, there is the punishment of sin to make up for either in this life or in Purgatory. The Good Thief had his chance to suffer on the cross, and we can only imagine what excruciating pains crucifxion carries. Perhaps, too, God dealt more leniently with him, in this very hour of the Redemption, in canceling all his debt of temporal punishment and promising him immediate entry into paradise.

Ezechiel was told by God: "*As* I live . . . I desire not the death of the wicked, but that the wicked turn from his way, and live." (*Ez.* 33:11). Through Isaias, God spoke these words: "Can a woman forget her infant, so as not to have pity on the son of her womb? And if she should forget, yet will not I forget thee." (*Is.* 49:15). *Psalm* 102, which concerns God's mercy, says: "As a father hath compassion on his children, so hath the Lord compassion on them that fear him: for he knoweth our frame. He remembereth that we are dust." (*Ps.* 102:13-14). God compares Himself to both a mother and a father in telling of His care for a soul. The book of *Ecclesiasticus* sums it up: "For according to his greatness, so also is his mercy with him." (*Ecclus.* 2:23).

Imagine the greatness of God as you see it in the great world He created, in the magnitude of mountain and ocean, in the vastness of space, in the far-flung distance of stars. As great as all this . . . is God's mercy. Christ on the Cross showed this mercy in action by the words: "This day thou shalt be with me in paradise."

Good Thief Not Isolated Case

Since the Good Thief, there have been countless similar stories of deathbed conversions, of souls saved at the last minute through the great mercy of God. No doubt there are many of whom we never hear, for the conversion may only be a silent act of perfect contrition, known only to the person concerned, and to God.

In 1907, a man lay dying in the hospital of Lucca, Italy. He was not only a publicly known sinner, but he was also a man who had openly fought against religion. The Sisters in the hospital tried to do their duty by urging him to repent, but without success. The Capuchin Fathers in charge of the hospital did the same thing. They too had no success. Finally they called in the pastor of the parish in which the man lived. Many people advised this priest not even to try to come, seeing how rudely the patient had shoved off the Sisters and the other priests. The pastor came anyway, but his words were also in vain, as predicted. "I have never believed in these sham terrors of yours, and I don't know who this Christ is of whom you speak. Heaven indeed! Hell indeed! Leave me in peace and let no one come again to bother me with such ridiculous proposals." In this vein the dying man spoke.

His pastor went home greatly afflicted. But as he entered his room, his eyes fell on the book he had just started reading, *The Life of Gemma Galgani.* He knelt down, and with tears he besought Gemma's aid.

At 11 p.m., the pastor asked his chaplain to go to the hospital in the company of a woman who was an acquaintance of the dying man, to see what might yet be done. The hospital allowed only the woman to go in. Hardly had she entered the man's room and begun to talk than he asked for a priest. The priest entered the room. The sinner made a good, humble Confession, was anointed, and received Viaticum. He died a few hours later, about 4 a.m. When the Holy Father of the time, now known as St. Pius X, heard of this conversion, he was very greatly moved.

St. Thérèse, the Little Flower, once heard of a

man condemned to death who refused to repent. He would have nothing to do with the prison chaplain. She began to offer up her sacrifices and prayers for him. But on the day of execution this man walked out to the gallows still refusing the ministration of the Church. A priest went along, hoping that at the last minute the prisoner might change his mind and repent. But the condemned man went steadfastly on. He waited for the noose to be put around his neck. Then, in the last instant, before the trap was sprung, he grasped the crucifix from the priest's hand and kissed it. Evidently the mercy of God had pursued him to the last and granted him the grace of this final act of contrition, even though he had refused the Sacraments. Such a sign would be sufficient warrant for the attending priest to administer Last Anointing afterwards (in the hope that life is still present). This sign may have indicated perfect contrition, transforming the darkness of sin into the light of grace.

Even where it seems that there could be no hope, there God's mercy still may stretch. The story is told of a man who committed suicide by leaping off a bridge. His daughter was more upset by the thought of his eternal damnation than she was overwhelmed by sorrow at his death, though she loved him dearly. He had not been faithful to his religion in his later years. She had prayed and prayed, begging God to have mercy on his soul, both before and after his death. Finally, she was assured by a saintly person that her father had been saved. Between the bridge and the water the man had repented. There was only a flash of time. The muddy waters and the flames of Hell were equally close. But before the waters of the river swallowed him up, the waters of grace poured into his soul. He had an instant in which to turn to God in perfect contrition.

Repentance Must Be Freely Willed

Now the question might occur: How is it that some still go to Hell, despite the great mercy of God? The answer is bound up in the mystery of free will decisions and God's justice. God will await the free will of man. His mercy is there, but man must co-operate by freely repenting. Christ waited on the Cross for the expression of sorrow on the part of the thief before promising him salvation. He must have been waiting also for the same from the thief on His left, and would gladly have given the same reply to him, but the other did not repent.

If a man does not repent after mortal sin, God's justice demands that he must be punished in Hell. God does not force man to love Him.

We Can Help

It is true, however, that God lets the prayers and tears and sacrifices of others have an influence on the conversion of mortal sinners. In the cases just recalled, the pastor, priests, nuns, St. Thérèse, the man's daughter, were greatly interested in the salvation of the sinners involved and did all possible for their conversion. We recall the words of Our Lady of Fatima in this connection. She said that many souls go to Hell because there is no one to pray and make sacrifices for them.

Do We Help?

It is surprising to see the indifference of friends and relatives concerning the soul of one who is living outside of the Church. "Yes, he has been outside for years," they will say and simply shrug their shoulders. Even when the person is dying, often no effort is made to arouse him to faith and repentance. He is labelled as a hopeless case. Friends and relatives put on him the seal of Judas without making an effort to help. They may not even notify a priest, thinking it to be of no use. To act in this way is simply not to understand the mercy of God. Likewise, it is to underestimate the power of prayer and personal sacrifice for bringing about the conversion of another.

We Should Rejoice at a Sinner's Return

Even worse than indifference is the attitude of taking offense when somebody who has been outside of the Church returns at the end of his life and is given Christian burial. The one who murmurs about this is like the older brother of the Prodigal Son. When he heard the music and found out his father had killed the fattened calf because the younger son had returned, he was angry and would not go into the house. He stated his grievance: "Behold, for so many years do I serve thee, and I have never transgressed thy commandment, and yet thou hast never given me a kid to make merry with my friends." (*Luke* 15:29). His father answered him: "Son, thou art always with me, and all I have is thine. But it was fit that we should make merry and be glad, for this thy brother was dead and is come to life again; he was lost, and is found."

Just before telling the story of the Prodigal Son, which is a story of God's mercy for the sinner, Our Lord had told of the lost sheep. (*Luke* 15:4 ff.). "What man of you that hath an hundred sheep: and if he shall lose one of them, doth he not leave the ninety-nine in the desert, and go after that which was lost, until he find it? . . . I say to you, that even so there shall be joy in heaven upon one sinner that doth penance, more than upon ninety-nine just who need not penance."

Save a Soul

All of us ought to be co-operators with God in saving souls. If we were interested enough, and prayed and sacrificed enough, we might be the means of having one more person get to Heaven. Pick out someone who has fallen by the wayside; make sure his parish priest knows about him, and keep that person in your prayers; do things by way of sacrifice for him.

Never Give Up

The devil, as we know, never gives up, even on Saints, tormenting them, tempting them to death itself. We ought never to give up on sinners. Somebody has used the expression, "to make a shoestring catch of souls." This is taken from baseball and refers to a fly ball being caught just off the ground. Why not be a fielder for God? Make a great run for some soul that seems out of reach, and see if you cannot make a shoestring catch. Such a catch is big news when it saves a game; it is the best of news when it saves a soul. Christ still waits to say: "This day thou shalt be with me in paradise." But He must wait for free repentance. In the inscrutable designs of God, we can have a hand in this through prayer and sacrifice.

∽ **THIRD WORD** ∽

"When Jesus therefore had seen his mother and the disciple standing whom he loved, he saith to his mother: Woman, behold thy son. After that, he saith to the disciple: Behold thy mother."

—*John* 19:26-27

Our Sorrowful Mother

THE mother of a newborn child, especially if it is her first child, is a very happy person. Let us suppose that this happy mother, as is usually the case, comes to the church for the Baptism. Again this is an occasion of joy: the first visit of the child to the church, his rebirth in the Sacrament of Baptism. In the midst of all this joy, however, suddenly there comes a warning of great sorrow. Somebody steps forward and predicts that the child will one day bring extreme pain of spirit to the mother.

It is easy to imagine the effect this would have, even though the prediction were made by somebody who was just taking a wild guess or trying to cause a scene. Were it made by a person known for his holiness of life, it might well hurt far more deeply.

25

Simeon Speaks

This is what happened on the occasion of the Infant Jesus' first visit to the Temple in Jerusalem. He was taken there by Mary and Joseph—not for Baptism, of course, but to be presented according to the Mosaic Law. It was on this occasion that the young mother heard the words of a sorrowful prophecy concerning her child. An aged man who was just and devout took the Infant into his arms and thanked God that he had lived to see this day. Then he spoke to Mary: "Behold this child is set for the fall, and for the resurrection of many in Israel, and for a sign which shall be contradicted; and thy own soul a sword shall pierce." (*Luke* 2:34-35). These were the prophetic words of Simeon, a man well deserving to be believed because of his nearness to God.

The sky of the young mother had been bright with joy; now an ominous cloud of sorrow appears on the horizon. The shadow of this cloud will be ever present throughout the years. When Mary works in the house and hears the sound of childish laughter from without, there may come a twinge of pain. It is not of herself that she is thinking, but of Him. What will be the extent of His sufferings that they will make her own soul to be pierced? As the Child grows up and Mary rejoices, as all mothers do, at His development of mind and body, she still wonders how long off that day may be when the prophecy of Simeon will come true in its fullest extent.

Mary's Seven Sorrows

Simeon's words themselves were the point of the sword; the flight into Egypt and the loss of the Child for three days were deeper thrusts of the sword of sorrow. But the piercing of Mary's soul finally came on Good Friday.

Tradition counts seven chief sorrows of Mary. Four of them took place on Good Friday: the meeting with her Son on the way to Calvary; being present at the Crucifixion; the taking down of Our Lord's body from the Cross; and finally, His burial. Of Our Lady's grief on Calvary, St. Anselm says that it was more bitter than any bodily suffering.

A Mother at a Deathbed

Any mother worthy of the name suffers greatly at the deathbed of her child, especially if the dying child is in great pain. The mother, in her understanding and tender feeling, knows just what the child is going through, and she endures each pain with him. Quite often a good mother may say that she would rather suffer the pain herself than have her child suffer. Actually, both suffer, mother and child. The child suffers the physical pain in the body; the mother endures the same pain in her heart. The more love there is present, the more pain.

This is what happened on Calvary. Mary endured in her heart all that Christ suffered on the Cross. The measure of her love was the measure of her pain. We are not making any mistake in saying that no mother ever loved a child as Mary loved her Son. This is no mistake, because we know that no womanly heart was ever better made for loving than Mary's, and we know that no Son could ever inspire or deserve more love than Our Lord.

The purest, most unselfish souls can love best and suffer most. So we cannot really understand the depth of sorrow that was Mary's, because we do not have her selfless love. We can understand her interior martyrdom only in accord with the selfless love and sympathy of which our own souls are capable. Our general idea of what Mary went through will depend on our own depth of spirit.

In her heart, Our Lady felt the cutting words of mockery and derision. The hammer blows of the nails in the hands and feet rung in her head. As Our Lord moved in agony on the Cross, Mary endured the pain in her heart. Of both Christ and Mary we can use the words of Jeremias: "O all ye that pass by the way, attend, and see if there be any sorrow like to my sorrow." (*Lam*. 1:12).

Christ Willed It

St. Robert Bellarmine says that Our Lord willed that His Mother be present in His hour of infamy, shame and suffering in order to add to His own sufferings. He could have arranged things in such a way as to spare her this sorrow. But He did not spare her, nor did He spare Himself. To have her witness His last hours added to His own sufferings. We can understand this readily by asking ourselves what we would do to prevent someone dear from seeing us suffer. Many times people, especially if living at a distance, will go through operations and much sickness, and only when it is all over do they write to inform their relatives. Their idea is to spare those near and dear the pain of going through it with them and the worry about recovery. Our Lord could have spared Himself and His Mother the mutual grief of Good Friday, but He did not.

The Dying Son Provides

No, Mary was present at the Cross, and she was present in the mind of her Son. In the midst of accomplishing mankind's redemption, the Son did not forget to provide for His mother's future years on earth. He did not have insurance to leave, nor any material wealth. "The foxes have holes, and the birds of the air nests: but the son of man hath not where to lay his head." (*Matt.* 8:20). So He put His mother into the hands of a good friend. "Woman, behold thy son." And to St. John: "Behold thy mother."

St. John in his Gospel says that from that hour he took her "to his own." According to the Franciscan tradition, the Blessed Virgin Mary lived until the age of 72. Some of the time after Good Friday was spent at Jerusalem, some perhaps in Galilee to the north, some years at Ephesus. Finally, the Blessed Mother is said to have returned to Jerusalem, where she died. Historically speaking, however, it is difficult to be positive about these places, and likewise about her final age. We do know for certain that St. John took care of her, gladly fulfilling this sacred commission given to Him by the dying Saviour.

The fact that Our Lord asked John to care for His Mother is a sure sign that St. Joseph had already died. It also is a strong proof that Mary had no other sons to look after her. If she had, St. John would not have been asked to stand in the place of a son to her.

St. John's Unique Role

St. John the Apostle was undoubtedly given a most wonderful treasure, a most enviable trust, when Mary was placed in his care. He might be called a second St. Joseph, since the duties of St. Joseph in caring for the Blessed Mother fell upon him.

The fact that he, and not some other, received this charge was not by accident. He had the necessary qualities and virtues to receive such a sacred commission. St. Jerome says that it was especially in view of his virginity that he was chosen. The virgin Son gave the virgin Mother to a man who was a virgin. John is the one Apostle of whom we are sure that he was not married. He had chosen the state of virginity, most likely at the urging of the Master Himself. He was the beloved disciple, who at the Last Supper rested on the breast of Christ.

St. John had been the favorite on other occasions. Along with Peter and James he had seen Jesus transfigured on Mt. Thabor. (*Mark* 9). He had, with the same two Apostles, been present in Gethsemani during Our Lord's agony. He and his brother James had been called by Our Lord the "Sons of Thunder," perhaps because of their zeal in wanting to call down vengeance on a town that would not receive Him. (*Luke* 9:54). Later, John was anything but a Son of Thunder, for he wrote lyrically of the love of God and neighbor, and in his old age he is said to have preached always the same sermon: "My little children, love one another."

This, then, was the man favored so signally, the man to whom the Virgin Mother was committed on Calvary. He had already received many special favors, but nothing to match the mark of affection and confidence that went to him on the afternoon of the Redemption.

Our Mother Too

We might perhaps be inclined to a kind of holy "envy" of St. John the Apostle in receiving Mary to care for as his mother. But in reality we have all received her as our Mother. This beautiful, further interpretation of Christ's words has gained favor from at least the twelfth century; many popes have written of it as being the common belief of the Church. Christ's words without doubt were meant, in the first place, to provide for His Mother. But He was also leaving her to us as our Mother and asking her to look on all men as her children. John stood in our place; he represented mankind. All men were thus asked to look up to Mary as their spiritual Mother, and she in turn was asked to see in everybody her spiritual child.

She Cares for Each One

Undoubtedly Mary is fulfilling her part as the Mother of all grace. She is fulfilling her part in giving loving attention to the children of men. She is well able to do this, since she has a heart big enough for all, just as the mother of a large family has a heart big enough to love each child. She is able to act as a mother to all, since she has a mother's feelings for all. It makes no difference to her whether you are rich or poor, beautiful or plain, old or young. Neither does it make any difference what color your skin is.

In each person she can see someone for whom Christ her Son suffered and died. In each soul she can see the possibility of a more perfect formation in the image of God. Her maternal solicitude and care go further, down to the same details that we ourselves are interested in as a matter of daily life. She knows of and cares about our smaller hopes and fears, our domestic problems, the state of our health. She can measure every pain because she has felt them all. She can understand each heartache because they were all contained in the great agony of Calvary.

Modern Evidence

We have living proof of her motherly care in the great shrines at Loreto, Lourdes, Fatima, Guadalupe and other places. Each of these tells its own story of her interest in the children of men. At Lourdes, for example, her care for those with afflictions is well attested. Many there have obtained help in sickness and disease.

At Lourdes there has been for many years a commission of medical men who study the reports of cures. Any qualified doctor—Catholic, non-Catholic, even atheist—is allowed to serve on this board, to go over the reports and to give his findings. Between 1,500 and 2,000 doctors every year examine the sick and check on reported cures at the Lourdes Medical Bureau. Since the first cure on February 28, 1858, of four-year-old Justin Bouhohorts from tuberculosis, down through 1955, the Medical Bureau had approved 1,862 cases as instances of remarkable healing. When a cure is completely beyond any explanation known to medical science, the doctors simply say that the event is from a cause beyond their knowledge. They do not necessarily call it a miracle, and neither does the Church, for the Church is extremely cautious and uses the word *miracle* only rarely. But whatever we call these extraordinary cases of regained health, the important point is that Mary shows herself interested in her children, even as regards the health of the body. Her intercessory power at such a place as Lourdes cannot be denied. She is the watchful, loving Mother who has the interests of her children at heart. Principally, of course, she has at heart their spiritual interests; but she also does not pass over with an unseeing glance their material needs.

She Does Not Let Us Down

Many Catholics readily testify to their devotion to Mary as their Mother. They will tell you that they have often experienced her help when in need, sometimes in ways that even surprised them. In the words of the *Memorare:* "Never was it known that anyone who fled to thy protection, implored thy help or sought thy intercession was left unaided." Mary is truly and always our Mother.

Take the Cue from St. John

It is up to us to become more and more Mary's sons and daughters. We might take the cue from St. John on how to do this. John was chosen because he was chaste and because he was present at the foot of the Cross. The more chaste we are and the more willing we are to participate in the Cross of Christ, the more are we worthy children of our Blessed Mother.

Practice Chastity

If God sends us the call to a life of chastity in religion or in the priesthood, that is a privilege that should be gladly accepted. If we remain in the world, single or married, the practice of chastity according to our state of life will endear us the more to our Blessed Mother. Every step toward impurity is a step away from her; every step toward purity, every effort made to preserve purity means to come closer to knowing and loving Mary, the lily of purity.

Stand at the Cross

We must also be willing to stand at the foot of the Cross. Every life brings its burden and cares. It is easy to rebel against these, to develop self-pity, to murmur at our lot. Most lives have their share of sickness, either personal or in those for whom one is responsible. Again, this can be the source of dissatisfaction and bitterness. To take these things in the proper spirit, to unite our sufferings with those of Our Lord is to stand at the foot of the Cross as St. John did. When we stand there, we are in a better position to hear the words: "Behold thy mother." And there Mary is in a better position to see us as her children.

No doubt most of us want to be closer to Mary, to have a greater love for her, more devotion to her, but we feel deficient. It may not be a bad idea to take this cause to St. John. Pray to him for a greater devotion to the Blessed Virgin Mary. Ask him for help to learn how to love chastity, to be willing to stand at the foot of the Cross. Such a prayer cannot fail to be answered immediately. Into our lives will come the richness of being true children of the greatest of all mothers.

∽ FOURTH WORD ∽

"And about the ninth hour Jesus cried with a loud voice, saying: *Eli, Eli, lamma sabacthani?* that is, My God, my God, why hast thou forsaken me?"

—*Matt.* 27:46

Desolation of Christ On the Cross

OF THE seven words of Christ on the Cross, the first three were said in the early part of the afternoon. The last four words were uttered shortly before His death about 3 o'clock. For the greater part of His time on the Cross, no words of Christ are recorded by the Gospel writers. Was there silence during these hours? Did Our Lord, perhaps, pray inaudibly or in a low voice that could not be distinguished as He hung there suspended between heaven and earth?

It is thought that He prayed in the words of the *Psalms* that referred to His sufferings and death. The fourth word, in fact, is taken verbatim from *Psalm* 21 (22), being its opening verse. This *Psalm* was written by David and is a remarkable prophecy of the Redeemer.

A Mysterious Darkness

From the sixth to the ninth hour, that is, from noon until 3 o'clock, there was darkness over the whole land. When the Son of God was dying, the very elements went into mourning. This strange midday darkness was noticed also by at least two writers other than the Evangelists. St. Denis experienced this phenomenon in Heliopolis, a city of Egypt. And a Greek writer and historian, Phlegon, says that in the fourth year of the 202nd Olympiad there took place a greater and more extraordinary eclipse than had ever happened before, "for at the sixth hour the light of day was changed into the darkness of night, so that the stars appeared in the heavens."

The darkness evidently extended not only over Palestine but at least for some hundreds of miles farther. It was a strange darkness, not caused by an ordinary eclipse. The moon at the time was full, and a full eclipse can occur only at the new moon. But, even if this were an eclipse of the sun by the moon, it would have caused darkness only for a few minutes, not for three hours. We do not know the exact physical causes of the obscuring of the sun on Good Friday. God, who made nature, could certainly have created various conditions to keep back the sun's light during the agony of His Son on Calvary.

Enemies Did Not Repent

One might think that this mystifying darkness would make the enemies of Christ quake in fear and repent. Perhaps they were fearful, but they did not repent. They stifled their fear and hardened their hearts still further. They had not been convinced by the good life, the strong words, the miracles of Christ; so neither would this new sign convince them.

There is a terrible lesson here for all who would trample down the pangs of conscience. Start out on this course, and as time goes on there is no limit to the evil one can do and forget about. The human heart, when it is determined and directed deliberately into the way of evil, grows harder and harder. Blindness of mind keeps growing and growing, until only a miracle of God's grace can penetrate it.

Darkness Within

The darkness of night covered the land, a mysterious, unexplained darkness. In the soul of Him who suffered on the Cross there was an even more mysterious darkness. He was both God and man, yet the desolation of His spirit made Him cry out: "My God, my God, why hast thou forsaken me?" These words were spoken in Aramaic, the dialect of the people in that region. They were not spoken in an ordinary voice or whispered. Christ cried out in a loud voice.

Some of those who were standing by thought that He was calling on Elias, the prophet who had been taken up alive into Heaven. They said: "This man calleth Elias." Somebody in the crowd, perhaps moved to pity at this great cry of anguish, offered Him a sponge soaked in vinegar, extending it on a reed. But the others kept their old attitude of mockery and said: "Let be, let us see whether Elias will come to deliver him." (*Matt.* 27:49). Here again we can see the extent of the cruelty and the degree of hardness of which the human heart is capable as shown by those around the Cross. After witnessing His suffering for all this time, the majority of those present could only offer a sneering remark—even to a dying man's heart-rending cry.

The Inner Darkness More Mysterious

The words of desolation of Christ on the Cross are the most difficult of all to understand. They are hard to understand because of the union of the humanity of Christ with His Divinity. How was it possible for Him who is God to feel Himself abandoned by God? According to some of the Saints who commented on this, the desolation of Christ, His feeling of abandonment, was the severest of all His sufferings. Although His words are certainly not words of despair, they are words that indicate the intensity of the entire ordeal through which the Saviour was going. He was just as Divine as ever, but His poor humanity was permitted to sink to the lowest depths of interior suffering.

In years to come, the martyrs would at times be so filled with joy during their tortures that their happiness shone through their faces. But it was not so with the Son of God. All feeling of support from His Father was withdrawn. His human feeling was so terrible that it brought forth the question: "Why hast thou forsaken me?"

Here on the Cross was Christ, rejected by the people of His own nation, forsaken by many of His closest friends. His body was one burning pain, one large agony. In His soul was overwhelming sorrow for the sins of the whole world. All these things crushed Him, weighed Him down. Yet added to this was the final, heavy, unbearable feeling of complete aloneness and abandonment.

All Doubt Removed

Perhaps we might have some doubt about the sufferings of Our Lord if He had not been reduced to the misery that brought forth His words of desolation. We might have imagined that the severity of His pains was nullified by the strength and joy that came from the union of His human nature with the Divine Nature. We might be tempted to think, "Maybe these sufferings were not nearly so hard for Him to bear as they would be for an ordinary person. After all, He was God." But once we have heard and pondered over the fourth word from the Cross, we know that what Christ

endured was not any easier because He was also
God. He went the whole way; He stopped at nothing in drinking to its dregs the bitter cup of complete suffering of body and soul.

His Desolation Is Our Consolation

In undergoing this desolation and in letting us
know about it, Our Lord has provided great consolation for all who must suffer, and especially for
all who feel discouraged and forsaken. Any person
who has much to endure and perhaps feels
enveloped by the darkness of despondency, who
feels completely alone in his pain, can always
think of Jesus on the Cross and His cry of abandonment. As long as faith endures, those words of
Our Lord will bring consolation.

Discouragement

There is an old story about a boy who started
out carrying a young calf a certain distance each
day. He kept at this, and as the calf grew, he was
able to keep carrying it because he himself was
growing stronger. But finally the day came when
he could no longer lift the animal. It was just too
heavy.

Sickness or any trouble that lasts a long time is
like a calf that keeps growing. We can put up with
it for a day, for a week, or for a few weeks, but
finally the time often comes when it appears to be
too heavy to bear. In reality, the sickness or trou-

ble may not be any worse, but the heaviness of discouragement is upon it, and that is what makes it seem so impossible to bear. This discouragement is actually worse than the malady itself.

A Great Enemy

Discouragement is the great enemy of the human spirit. Despondency is the great enemy of souls. If we can speak of the devil being happy, he is "happy" when people give in to the complete unhappiness of discouragement and despondency. Our Lord on the Cross knew this, so He let us know that He too had to fight to the last ounce of His human endurance to preserve courage and strength of spirit. He let us know this, that we might turn to Him and find the courage we need in our severest difficulties.

United with Christ for Courage

Many people who are chronically ill have found strength and even joy in suffering because they suffer in union with Christ. There are in the United States at least two societies with nationwide membership of sick people united with one another and with Christ in offering up their sufferings. The members of these organizations are not all flat on their backs. Some are invalids, some semi-invalids whose activities are limited by disease or weakness. All have one thing in common: their illnesses are chronic. They have the long, hard pull against discouragement. By offering up their sufferings for the conversion of sinners, for peace, for the needs of others and for personal sanctification, a great amount of good is done. At the same time, by union with Our Lord in mind and heart, the enemies of despair and despondency are kept at a distance.

The Despondency of Sameness

Discouragement, however, is not reserved for those with chronic sickness or extraordinary troubles of some other kind. The wear and tear of everyday life can weaken a person's inner spirit. In a popular song, the poor fellow who digs sixteen tons of coal a day must evidently be healthy to do so much strenuous work. But he sings a dirge of forlornness; he feels that he has "sold his soul to the company store," for all he can do is work and then spend his money to pay for the necessities of life. There are many who feel that they keep working and working and do not get anywhere. Then when some small additional trouble comes up, it can become the proverbial "straw that breaks the camel's back" and may result in complete despondency.

Spiritual Aridity

There is a special kind of discouragement that plagues the person who is trying hard to lead a good spiritual life. His prayers may seem never to have anything in them. They are like an old record. There is no sweetness, no sensible consolation. They seem like just so many words, almost without meaning. God hardly seems real any more. He is at a distance, not close. A person who feels this way must remember that he is no more abandoned by God than was Christ on the Cross.

The feeling of God's nearness and the enjoyment of our prayers to Him have nothing to do with reality, nor with the value of the prayers. Some food that is tasteless or even bitter may be far better for us than that which delights the sense of taste. In the same way, prayer may be tasteless or even burdensome and yet may be of more value than that which is sweet and consoling. God never actually abandons us, but He may allow us to feel that way, even as God the Son Himself felt abandoned on Calvary.

In the lives of many Saints, we find that they were at times completely without consolation in their prayers. St. John of the Cross even uses the expression *"The Dark Night of the Soul"* to describe the condition of very holy and chosen souls whom God allows to feel absolutely cut off from Himself. St. Thérèse, the Little Flower, tells us in her autobiography that during most of her life she felt very dry in her prayers. St. Margaret of Cortona at one time felt so much fear and despair that she would not receive Holy Communion until commanded by her confessor. Some Saints have felt so completely cut off from God that they imagined they would surely lose their souls. This they felt despite leading lives of heroic self-denial and prayer.

But the Saints and all holy people understand the lesson of Our Lord's cry of abandonment from the Cross. If Christ in the very act of accomplishing mankind's redemption felt forsaken, why should not *they* sometimes feel cut off from God, despite their good works and prayers?

Dryness Teaches Us: Seek God for His Sake

In the early years of our life, or if we have been converts, perhaps in the early years of conversion, God gives us the grace of much joy in prayer and in the reception of the Sacraments. We feel so much better after going to Confession and receiving Communion. But as time goes on, this sweetness and consolation disappear. At such a time we should not give up or succumb to the thought that our good practices and works are useless. They are every bit as good as before. They may be and most likely are of even more value, for we can be sure that now we seek God for His own sake and not for the sake of the pleasure in it that there may be for ourselves.

An Uphill Battle

Our age is an age that wants quick results. Whatever is done—building a home or church, getting an education, learning a trade—must be done as swiftly as possible. We may carry this spirit over into our relations with God. We would like to establish satisfying relations rapidly with Him, save our souls with a few efforts, and then coast on. But things do not work that way. Saving one's soul is an uphill battle. Our perseverance may be tried and tested in many ways, even to feeling cut off from God Himself.

If this happens, or *whatever* happens to discourage us, we must never give up.

Our age is also an age of sentimentality. Religion is made a matter of *feeling good* about God and all that pertains to Him. It is taken for granted that God will fill with consolation those who try to do His Will. But this is not always the case. In practicing our religion, we must remember Calvary and the desolation of Christ on the Cross. God may try our souls to their depths. We must remember the great truth that though we may *feel* forsaken by God, we are never actually forsaken. The Saviour Himself felt forsaken by God, leading Him to cry out those mysterious words: "My God, my God, why hast Thou forsaken me?" But God is close to us, even as He was to Christ.

∽ FIFTH WORD ∽

"Afterwards, Jesus knowing that all things were now accomplished, that the scripture might be fulfilled, said: I thirst."
—*John* 19:28

Christ's Thirst for Souls

IT was customary to prepare a drink for criminals about to be crucified. This was usually done by women who were friends of the one about to be executed or by women of compassionate heart who lived in the vicinity. The drink consisted of wine mixed with bitter ingredients such as myrrh and aloes, and its purpose was to act as an anesthetic to deaden the pain.

When Our Lord first arrived on Calvary, before being nailed to the Cross, He was offered such a drink. Most likely it had been prepared by some of the women who had been His followers. He tasted it, but would not drink. He thus afforded those who had made it the consolation of knowing that He had sipped the drink. But He did not take enough to lessen His pain. He wanted to suffer with full consciousness.

Later, just shortly before He died, Our Lord uttered the words, "I thirst." It was then that someone—probably a soldier—dipped a sponge into the mixture of vinegar and water that was there and extended it on a stalk of hyssop to the lips of the dying Saviour. This vinegar and water was available at the scene of execution because it served to slake the thirst of the soldiers.

It seems that the act of giving this liquid on a sponge to Christ was a slight act of mercy. Some of those standing by spoke up against even this, saying: "Let be, let us see whether Elias will come to deliver him." (*Matt.* 27:49). But the man extending the sponge went ahead, and Our Lord accepted the proffered refreshment. (*John* 19:30).

Thirst Is Torture

Thirst was one of the great agonies of crucifixion. It was caused by the loss of blood, by fever and by general exhaustion. Thirst accompanies any severe, drawn-out pain. It can become worse than the original pain that causes it. According to St. Robert Bellarmine, St. Emmeram, when tied to a stake and tortured, complained only of thirst. Men at sea who go for a long time without water have become raving maniacs because of their thirst. Anybody who has suffered a fever knows something of the agony of thirst. In fact, even a healthy person on a hot day can become almost desperate for something to drink. Thirst, then, was one of the sufferings of Our Lord upon the Cross.

Not a Plea for Comfort

Our Lord's words came at the very end, just before His death. Therefore they were not a plea to alleviate the thirst itself. He had endured the long time on the Cross without drink, refusing that which was offered to Him at first. After enduring this suffering to the end, He finally said: "I thirst," in order to acquaint us with the fact of this additional suffering and to fulfill an Old Testament prophecy—as St. John says: "that the scripture might be fulfilled." The Scripture referred to was from *Psalm* 68:22 (69:22): "and in my thirst they gave me vinegar to drink."

A Deeper Meaning

In his explanation of this *Psalm*, St. Augustine says that there was another reason why Christ said the words: "I thirst." St. Augustine says that these words showed not only the Saviour's desire for drink, but also—and still more—the desire with which He was inflamed, that His enemies might believe in Him and be saved. Our Lord thus desired so greatly the good and the salvation of the Jewish people that His longing can be well described as a thirst. One who wants something intensely is said to thirst for it. For example, a person may thirst for knowledge or for fame.

Just a few days previously, Our Lord had entered Jerusalem in triumphal procession. As He drew near and saw the city, He had wept over it, saying: "If thou also hadst known, and that in this thy day, the things that are to thy peace; but now they are hidden from thy eyes . . . because thou hast not known the time of thy visitation." (*Luke* 19:42-44). Our Lord had wept over the city of Jerusalem because it would be destroyed (by the Romans in 70 A.D.) and its people would suffer much in the next generation, and ever after, as a punishment for not accepting Him. He wept over the souls that would be lost due to their stubbornness and hardheartedness. His longing for the souls of His people was also expressed when He had lamented: "Jerusalem, Jerusalem, that killest the prophets, and stonest them that are sent to thee, how often would I have gathered thy children as the bird doth her brood under her wings, and thou wouldst not?" (*Luke* 13:34).

Jesus Thirsts for All Souls

Our Lord thirsted for the souls of His own people, the members of the Jewish race. He thirsted also for the souls of all mankind. In the seventeenth century, when He appeared to St. Margaret Mary, He said: "Behold this Heart which has so loved men that it has spared nothing to testify its love for them, even to exhausting and consuming itself for their sake. But in return for this I receive nothing from the generality of mankind but ingratitude. . . ."

The Heart of Jesus is a great Heart, full of love, looking for love in return, so that souls may be

saved and come to Heaven. Our Lord also said to
St. Margaret Mary: "My Heart is so full of love for
men that it can no longer contain within itself the
fire of charity." Thus we may expand the interpretation of St. Augustine and apply the words "I
thirst" to express Our Lord's longing for the love
of all mankind and for the salvation of all souls.

Why He So Thirsted

A soul—each soul—is precious. Its value cannot be measured in material terms. The world
itself is not worth one soul. There is simply no
comparison between an immortal soul, capable of
loving God for all eternity, and the treasures of
earth. This is as things appear to the eye of God
in their true value. Likewise, from the viewpoint
of man himself, there can be no comparison
between gaining untold wealth or pleasure or
power, and the saving of his own soul. No one has
put this truth more clearly than Our Lord Himself when He asked the question: "For what doth
it profit a man, if he gain the whole world, and
suffer the loss of his own soul?" (*Matt.* 16:26).

Christ hanging on the Cross knew the immea-
surable value of each soul in itself. He knew how
much it meant for each person to save his soul
and be happy in praising and loving God for eternity. So His great love reached out to each person,
and His great Heart longed for the eternal happiness of each person. He thirsted for souls.

Our Own Incredible Blindness

It is one of the mysteries of life why so many people in practice put such a slight value upon their souls. It is a mystery of blindness, perversity and shortsightedness.

Whatever is regarded as precious is guarded. Money is put into safes with complicated locks. Jewels are placed in vaults. Health is a matter of daily concern. When something goes wrong or seems wrong with bodily health, the doctor is straightway consulted. Vitamin charts are studied; people who have to lose weight check on their calories. They do a very good job of fasting, much better than most do during Lent. Insurance is kept up on items of property that could be suddenly destroyed or damaged, such as homes and autos. Yet the man who would not think of taking out a car in traffic without insurance may think nothing of living in mortal sin, when an accident or a sudden sickness could immediately block out consciousness and result in death without a chance of obtaining forgiveness, and thus bring eternal damnation.

People who would be frightened to death at taking a chance on using a weak ladder, or crossing a condemned bridge, take all kinds of chances with their souls. They balance on the constantly unraveling rope of life, while below lie the flames of Hell. They are the real daredevils in the strict sense of the word, for a sudden slip from or break in the rope of life—and they will belong to the devil for eternity. It is indeed a mystery how people can be so shortsighted in regard to the value of their immortal souls.

Your Soul First

We can overcome this shortsightedness by keeping our eyes fixed on the Cross of Christ, by reflecting on all He did to save the souls of men, by considering His yearning love for each person.

First of all, each of us has his own soul to take care of. The needs of our own soul must be placed in the position of priority over all bodily needs. If there is a conflict, the soul must never come out in second place.

It may happen that there is a deadly disease wasting our souls—a habit of frequent mortal sin against which our efforts have been only half-hearted. This deadly disease must by all means be conquered, no matter what the cost. Our Lord advised: "If thy hand, or thy foot scandalize [provide an occasion of sin to] thee, cut it off, and cast it from thee. It is better for thee to go into [eternal] life maimed or lame, than having two hands or two feet, to be cast into everlasting fire. And if thy eye scandalize thee, pluck it out, and cast it from thee. It is better for thee having one eye to enter into life, than having two eyes to be cast into hell fire." (*Matt.* 18:8-9).

Here is the answer to those who think they must sinfully limit a family; to those who are invalidly married and therefore living in constant mortal sin; to those who habitually commit grievous sin of any kind. No matter what it costs, no matter what must be torn asunder, though it be as close as a hand or foot or eye—all must go when in conflict with the interests of one's immortal soul. There can be no value so precious—whether economic, or pertaining to human affection, or anything whatsoever—as the value of one's soul.

A man who was sick and pretty well up in years once remarked that it was only when he was about fifty years old that he first realized forcefully that one day he must die and meet his judgment. The sooner we too realize this, perhaps the sooner will we realize that ultimately the only lasting values are those that are spiritual and that pertain to God and our souls.

We Are Keepers of Our Brothers' Souls

In our care for our own souls, however, we must not forget the souls of others. We are told to love our neighbor as ourselves. (*Matt.* 22:39). In part, this refers to bodily needs, but it refers in particular to the spiritual needs of the soul.

Since our first obligations are toward those who are closest to us, we have to take into consideration the souls of members of our own families. We may not repeat the question of Cain: "Am I my brother's keeper?" (*Gen.* 4:9). In a quite definite way we are responsible for the salvation of husband or wife, son and daughter, brother and sister, friend and neighbor.

Parents usually recognize that they have an

obligation to provide for the spiritual welfare of their children. But not all, of course, do as well as they might in this regard, making the mistake of overemphasizing physical and educational care. For instance, some parents are quite exacting about school grades, requiring that their children work hard at their studies. But they think little of allowing the children to miss their religious instructions, or they do little to encourage regular attendance at Mass and reception of the Sacraments. The home is well heated and drafts are abhorred. Yet questionable books and magazines are permitted to chill innocent fervor, and worse. The Holy Name of God may be heard more often in expressions of anger than in words of prayer. The walls of the house are clean and tastefully decorated, yet the strong spirit of faith and of confidence in God does not pervade the home because the parents' values are much more consciously material than spiritual. Thus, parents technically recognize their obligation of providing for the spiritual welfare of their children, but actually do little about it.

Still less do husband and wife recognize their obligation toward each other's spiritual welfare. The husband recognizes his duty to provide for the family; the wife her duty of home-making. But they may fail to see that their main duty *to each other* is to help the other party obtain eternal salvation. Two people who live as closely together and share life as much as husband and wife cannot but have a definite effect on the supernatural destiny of each other.

So it is with all who share life together as relatives and friends. They do have an effect one upon the other. If we have the proper outlook on the value of souls, our influence cannot be anything but good.

Interest in Souls Must Be Universal

One whose heart beats in union with the Sacred Heart of Jesus can never forget the spiritual good of all other people. He will pray for those who have fallen away from the Church; he will pray for the conversion of men to the true Faith. He will make sacrifices in order that all men may come to the knowledge of the truth and to the grace of the seven Sacraments.

In a way, one who thirsts for souls is always working for them. He is like a businessman who is always trying to improve his business, who uses every opportunity to establish friendly relations or to pick up useful information. The real businessman does not miss any opportunities. Neither will one who is truly interested in the salvation of souls miss any opportunities. To think differently, to act from any weaker principle, is to refuse to slake the thirst of Christ.

Using an Organized Method

The Crusade for Souls spearheaded by Fr. John A. O'Brien in the mid-20th century was an example of what can be done for souls by an organized group effort. The Crusade harnessed the energies of thousands of workers and guided them in a door to door campaign. It was a shoe-leather apostolate. In some instances, it was carried out on a diocesan-wide scale; or again, the dioceses of a state united in the campaign, as was done in Indiana in 1956 and Wisconsin in 1957; or the dioceses of several states united, as was contemplated in Oregon, Montana and Idaho in 1958. The aim was to visit all the homes in the territory, thus finding those who have lapsed from the Faith and inviting them back, and interesting those of no religion in the Catholic Faith. The idea behind such a Crusade for Souls harmonizes with the wish of Christ expressed on the Cross when He said: "I thirst." This is a real and practical way to lead souls to Christ.

We Can Help

Each of us will have opportunities of various kinds to help save souls and to win souls to the saving truths of the Faith. If we are really interested, we will learn how to explain and answer questions, or we will make available to those interested some little pamphlet on the subject. What a great amount of good might be done if we kept on hand a supply of pamphlets on key topics and handed them out as opportunity arose! We will always give a good example and live in such a way as to lead others to Christ. If we really love Christ, we will want the things that He wants.

With our whole soul, we will seek to help in whatever way we can so that souls may be saved.

In these ways all of us can answer the plea of Christ. Thus we may help to satisfy His great desire and thirst for the souls of all mankind.

✑ SIXTH WORD ✑

"Jesus therefore, when he had taken
the vinegar, said: It is consummated."
—*John* 19:30

The Task Is Finished

THE DEATH of a child or young person is
always an especially sad event. In them
the bloom of life was still fresh and unfold-
ing. Death in a young person seems to be the
denial of a promise; it seems to be the crushing of
an unfulfilled pledge of growth, development and
accomplishment. The sentiment of many is
expressed in the words: "It is a shame that he had
to die so young."

Sometimes death comes to a young father or
mother who have others dependent upon them.
They were anxious and willing to fulfill their
duties to their families, but the grim invitation to
quit this mortal life came, and they had to accept.
It happens at times that a priest is cut down in
the prime of life, perhaps shortly after ordination,
or after gaining a few years' experience. Ready
and glad though he was to go on with the work of
helping to save souls, he is forced to leave his task
unfinished.

So it is even with many in middle age whose lives are cut short. After long years of work and experience they were on the threshold of their most mature and productive years. With most people it takes time to acquire wisdom. Yet it seems that there is often but little time given to put the hard-won wisdom to practical use. Not many people in their forties or fifties care to say of their life and work: "It is finished."

Christ Declares His Work Done

Yet Christ on the Cross said those very words: "It is consummated." It is finished. He was in the prime of life, about 33 years of age. When He said, "It is finished," He did not mean merely that death was upon Him. He meant in the fuller sense that the task that had been given Him to do was done. He had accomplished His purpose in coming to earth. These words were the final expression of what He had said at the Last Supper: "I have glorified thee on the earth; I have finished the work which thou gavest me to do." (*John* 17:4).

When the laborer comes into his house after a hard day's work, he sits down and his mind runs back over the long hours of toil. He sighs contentedly, because he has finished the tasks of the day and can now rest. So Christ on the Cross looks back over the years of His life and especially over this past day. He has finished the work that was given Him. With the sense of having faithfully done all things, He can declare: "It is finished."

This was His sixth word on the Cross. Immediately after this He said His final word: "Father, into thy hands I commend my spirit," bowed His head and died.

Fulfills Prophecy

Just before uttering the words: "It is finished," Jesus had tasted of a drink that was held up to His lips on a stalk of hyssop. A soldier had dipped a sponge into the mixture of vinegar (derived from wine) and water, fastened the sponge to the stalk and held it up. At the beginning of the three hours on the Cross, Jesus had refused the drink, which might have alleviated His pain. Now when about to die, He tastes of the vinegar and thereby fulfilled the prophecy of *Psalm* 68:22: "And in my thirst they gave me vinegar to drink."

All That Was Written Was Accomplished

This was the last prophecy to be fulfilled before the last breath of Our Lord before He died. When He had set out for Jerusalem this last time, Christ had told the Apostles: "Behold, we go up to Jerusalem, and all things shall be accomplished which were written by the prophets concerning the Son of man." (*Luke* 18:31). One after another, the things that had been foretold were done. When Our Lord was nailed to the Cross and every last bone ached, the words of David were fulfilled:

"They have dug my hands and feet. They have numbered all my bones." (*Psalm* 21:17-18). All the prophecies had been fulfilled—from His conception by a virgin and His birth in Bethlehem (*Is.* 7:14 and *Mich.* 5:2) to the dividing of His garments by lot (*Psalm* 21:19) and His crucifixion with criminals (*Is.* 53:12). So Jesus could taste the vinegar and say in all truth: "It is finished."

Christ Was Not the Picture of Success

Let us take a look at the Man who says He has finished all that was assigned Him to do. He is anything but the picture of success as He makes the statement that His task is successfully concluded. The sky is dark, which may seem to indicate that this was indeed the dark hour for the work of Christ. Most of His supporters and friends were not to be seen. They had left in fear and in amazement at the turn of events in Our Lord's life.

Christ's enemies were triumphant; their plans to bring about His disgrace and death had been successful. They were the ones who mocked Him. He who had given so many devastating answers to them said nothing when they challenged Him to come down from the Cross if He were really the Son of God. (*Mark* 15:30). They even pointed to His miracles with contempt: "He saved others; let him save himself." (*Luke* 23:35). It certainly appeared to be their hour of triumph. It certainly looked as if He were a final failure.

Yet, as the earth began to quake, in the darkness and loneliness and shame and pain of the Cross, and not a minute away from death, Our Lord declared that His work was a success. "It is consummated." He had done all the things He had been sent to accomplish.

What He Could Have Done

Judging by worldly and material standards, we might well say: "What a shame for Him to die!" He was young. He could speak as no man ever had or ever would speak, to stir the minds and hearts of men and turn them to God. He could have continued to work miracles, thereby bringing comfort to many sick and crippled. He could have continued to instruct the Apostles. He could have gone on for thirty years as well as for three. Perhaps He could have written a book that might dissolve all religious doubt forever.

He could have gone to Rome, the center of the civilized world, as Peter and Paul did later and preached there the kingdom of God. Even if He eventually had to die for the salvation of mankind, why not at the age of sixty or sixty-five, after a full lifetime of His wonderful activities.

No matter what we may think, His work at the age of thirty-three was completed. Otherwise He would not have said: "It is consummated."

What Had He Accomplished?

Humanly speaking, everything looked bad. Yet Christ had completed His work of preaching and working miracles among His own people, the Hebrew nation. By His obedience He had atoned for the disobedience of Adam; by His humility He had counteracted the pride of all sinners. The gates of Heaven were re-opened. The Church had been founded to preserve truth and to administer the Sacraments, thereby bringing light and grace to save the souls of men. Perfect adoration and praise had been rendered to the majesty of God. So, as a worthy laborer with his task completed, Christ could say: "It is finished."

What about Our Own Sense of Values?

Thinking this over, we may well stop to realign our sense of values. It may be that we have a false set of values in our own lives. Maybe the things we think are so important are not very important at all. Maybe we are losing sight of why we are here on earth in the first place. There is no better place to think things over than in the shadow of the Cross, with the words of Christ ringing in our ears: "It is consummated."

Our Lame Excuses

Many times the excuse is given for missing Mass or devotions, or for not receiving Communion frequently: "I don't have time." This shows a false sense of values. There is time for everything else, but not for giving honor and glory to God, not for properly taking care of one's own soul. To say you don't have time means, in the last analysis, that you put a higher value on the other things that are taking up your time.

It is possible that even the daily morning and evening prayers are omitted quite regularly. Once in a while there may be a reasonable excuse. But to say: "I forget" is just another way of saying: "I don't think it is very important."

What Worries Me?

A way of checking on our sense of values is to ask ourselves what we worry about or are the most concerned about. What bothers us the most? Is it the state of our health? Is it the thought of establishing ourselves in an economically secure position? We should take care of our health; we should provide for our needs of food and shelter. But our main concern must always be our eternal salvation.

If a person consults a doctor about a persistent symptom and at the same time lives unconcernedly and blithely in the state of mortal sin, there is something wrong with his sense of values. He is worrying about preserving his life on earth, but in the meantime his soul is hanging over Hell, and it makes no impression on him. If a person makes a social blunder and frets over it because of what other people may think, yet at the same time commits mortal sin and does not care much what God thinks about it, his sense of values is wrong.

So the questions: "What bothers me? What do I worry about?" can give a good indication of where our highest values lie. For we are concerned over that which we value. We are concerned about losing a diamond, but not over a piece of glass. If the things of God and our own soul do not much concern us, then they are valued as a piece of glass. And if so valued, they are likewise trampled upon and cast aside as something of little worth.

Seek First God's Will

Our Lord told us not to be anxious about our food, or our clothing. "Be not solicitous therefore, saying, What shall we eat: or what shall we drink, or wherewith shall we be clothed? . . . For your Father knoweth that you have need of all these things. Seek ye therefore first the kingdom of God, and his justice, and all these things shall be added unto you." (*Matt.* 6:31-33).

If God takes care of the lilies of the field and the grass and the birds of the air, then He is certainly not forgetting us. Christ did not mean to encourage improvidence, but He wanted to tell us that we should rely on God more, to leave things up to Him, after we have done our reasonable part.

How foolish it is to break God's laws in an attempt to provide for material wants. To work needlessly on Sundays, to seek extra work on Sunday to earn a few more dollars shows lack of trust in God. Sinfully to limit one's family is the utmost foolishness; it means taking the burden on oneself and leaving nothing to God.

Each of Us Has a Task Assigned

Just as Our Lord came into the world with a task to do, so each one of us has a particular job to do in this world. We have our main purpose of life to fulfill, which is to know, love and serve God. That is the general purpose of all of us. No matter what our station in life, or what our age, we are each supposed to grow in the knowledge and love of God and come to serve Him better. But God also has given us a particular job to do, one that concerns us as individual persons. He has in mind some special way for us to serve Him, some special degree of love for us to arrive at while on this earth. There may be quite a number of small individual jobs for us to do, and when they are finished, then God calls us out of this life.

The biggest tragedy of life is to miss doing what God has sent us here to accomplish. The biggest mistake we can make in this life is to lay our plans with the question in mind: What can I get out of it? How can I get the most out of life for myself? Our question ought to be: How can I best do whatever it is God sent me here to do? What shall I do, so that when it is time to breathe my last breath I can say as Christ said: "It is consummated"?

It was no accident that Christ died on the

Cross. "He humbled himself, becoming obedient unto death, even to the death of the cross." (*Phil.* 2:8). He had said: "My meat is to do the will of him that sent me, that I may perfect his work." (*John* 4:34). That must be our question: How can I be obedient to the designs of God? Our food must be to do the holy Will of God.

How to Find Our Appointed Task

To discover what it is that God has in mind for us, we should start early in life, begging the Holy Spirit to direct us into the proper major vocation. Maybe God wants us to live in the married state, the single state, or the religious or priestly life. Usually He does not "force" us in any one direction. Few are knocked to the ground as was St. Paul and told by a heavenly voice to follow Christ as a priest and apostle.

To discover what God has in mind for us, we should also ask advice and guidance from a spiritual director, usually our regular confessor. If we are not interested enough to pray and to seek advice, then we may well enter the wrong vocation. At judgment, God will point out the work we did not accomplish upon the earth.

Do Not Come Down from the Cross

After we have chosen a vocation, we should live according to all the laws of God concerning our particular state: married, single, priestly or religious. The selfish single person will be asked on the day of judgment why he has not aided the needy, or devoted time to the care of parents, or helped in religious or charitable work. The careless priest will be told to look down and see the many souls left in ignorance and sin, whom he should have instructed and brought to repentance. The married who neglected their duties will have pointed out to them how their children were not taught the fear and love of God. They may have pointed out to them the work that some child of theirs should now be doing on earth—but that child was sinfully denied even existence. Where is this son of yours who should now be the assistant priest at this church? Look at these souls wandering without a shepherd.

To all alike will be pointed out this truth. The world taunted you: "Come down from the cross and save yourself." Unlike Christ, you tore yourself free from the cross of duty and tried to save yourself the pain and hardship of accomplishing your task on the earth. Therefore your work has not been finished. Before you breathed your last, you could not in truth say: "It is consummated."

It is not as difficult as might be imagined to find out what God wants us to do. If we are eager, and pray earnestly to do His will, to do our job in life; if we are faithful to the duties of each hour, God will enlighten us.

Each day we ought to pray with Christ: "Not my will, but thine be done." (*Luke* 22:42). We must be convinced that we are here to do God's Will, to accomplish some special job. Our job may be easy or hard, but whatever it is, God will see us through. At the end, like the weary laborer at the close of day, we will be able to look back over our day on earth and say: "Thank God the work is done." Like Christ on the Cross we will be able to say: "It is consummated. I have done the work You gave me to do."

⤳ SEVENTH WORD ⤳

"And Jesus crying with a loud voice, said: Father, into thy hands I commend my spirit. And saying this, he gave up the ghost."

—*Luke* 23:46

Leaving Things to God

IT WAS about 3:00 in the afternoon when Jesus said His last word and died. It had been a long time since the night before, when He had left the Upper Room to go to the Garden of Gethsemani. There had been about eighteen hours of uninterrupted stress and strain, agony of mind and pain of body. He had had no sleep the night before. The time after being apprehended in the Garden had been spent in going from court to court and being put on trial. He had gone from Annas to Caiphas, to Pilate, to Herod, and back to Pilate.

In between these trips, the soldiers had amused themselves by mocking Him, putting Him on a stump and placing a reed in His hand, as though He were king, then striking Him with the reed, spitting on Him, bending the knee before Him. Later in the morning, after He had been scourged, they had actually interwoven a crown of thorns and placed it on His head, again in derision of His claimed kingship. Then there had been the frenzied shouting, the overflowing of passion and hatred. It would have required nerves of steel not to be affected by all this clamor, especially when directed at oneself.

Beyond all this, moreover, was the heavy sorrow of knowing that these people, His own countrymen, had had every chance of knowing better. They had seen miracles and had heard the most convincing preaching. They had blinded themselves deliberately, even after the pagan judge, Pilate, had said that the man being tried was innocent.

Finally, Jesus had taken on His shoulder the heavy cross and had walked up the hill to Calvary, just outside the city wall. There He had been stripped of His garments and nailed with three large nails to the Cross. It does not take great imagination to realize the terrible pain of this nailing and the increased pain when He was raised on the Cross, attached by nails. There was no anesthetic, no pain-dulling "shot." He bore the raw pain without benefit even of the usual drink of wine and myrrh.

Crucifixion was considered even by the ancients, who were much rougher people than most of us are, as the most cruel form of death. The man on the cross alternated between two unbearable pains. He would slump until he could no longer get his breath, then would rise on the nail in his feet and support himself on this until the burning pain in the feet became unsupport-able, then he would slump again. When he no longer had the strength to rise, he suffocated. The loss of blood and the suffering would cause a fever, and this in turn would make the whole body ache and induce a great thirst.

This, then, was the suffering which Our Lord endured for three hours. And all this came at the end of a long night without sleep, a night of being dragged back and forth, falsely accused, mocked, browbeaten. It came after the scourging and crowning with thorns.

Interior Suffering

Besides this pain of the body, there was the deep anguish of Our Lord in thinking about the loss of many souls who would not profit from His sacrifice. He saw those gathered beneath the Cross who continued to ridicule Him to the end. He saw the people of all centuries who, in pride and disobedience and sensuality, would deliber-ately reject Him, His Church, His Law. Then there had been that most mysterious desolation of spirit leading Him to cry out, asking why God had forsaken Him. Truly He took upon Himself the full weight of sin, even to feeling cut off from God. As St. Paul says: "Wherefore it behoved him in all things to be made like unto his brethren, that he might become a merciful and faithful high priest before God, that he might be a propitiation for the sins of the people." (*Heb.* 2:17).

He Died Freely

The last words of Jesus were cried out with a loud voice. He had endured enough to cause death, but He was still the Master of life and death. Had He chosen, He could have gone on living. His loud cry and final words show that He died by His own choice. His voice was not the weak, hardly audible voice of one who has not an ounce of strength left. His words accepting death and His immediate bowing of His head thereafter show that He died because He willed to die.

At the moment of Christ's death there was a great earthquake. The rocks on Calvary were cleft, a rent appearing down the side of the hill. In Jerusalem, the great veil of the Temple that separated the Holy of Holies from the main part of the Temple was torn in two down the middle, signifying the end of the Old Law. The Roman centurion in charge of the soldiers, "seeing that crying out in this manner he had given up the ghost, said: Indeed this man was the son of God." (*Mark* 15:39). Many of the Jews left in fear and went back into the city, striking their breasts as a sign of submission to God.

Last Words Show Union with the Father

The last words of Jesus were words of trust in God, of resignation, love and confidence. "Father, into thy hands I commend my spirit." A little earlier He had cried out: "My God, my God, why hast thou forsaken me?" Those words show us the degree of bitterness and the depth of abandon-ment He experienced. But it would have been unthinkable that these words would be His last. No, His final words must show union and har-mony between the Son and the Father. Therefore, Jesus does not use the more distant form of address, "My God," but speaks familiarly, "Father."

Death is the final, lowest humiliation that the Saviour can undergo. Even at the end He could still have descended from the Cross, healed, and confounded all His enemies. He could have approached the point of death—yet without dying. But that was not the divine plan for Redemption.

Life is the sweetest and best of all the gifts of God. No one ever realized this more than Our Lord. But He now gladly gave up this life, accept-ing the final humiliation of death in love and sub-mission to the will of His Father. That is the meaning of the words: "Into Thy hands I commend my spirit." They are words of complete resignation to the will of God. Life comes from God; life must be used for Him; life must go back to Him.

When We Should Use Christ's Words

There are three times especially when we should ourselves use the words: "Into Thy hands I commend my spirit."

First, we should use them each evening as part of our night prayers. When night comes and another day is over, so is another part of our life on earth. Each day is a miniature life in itself. Each time a person lies down to sleep, he gives up conscious control of life. Sleep is an imitation of death, so that we sometimes even speak of death as a long sleep. Here, then, is a good time to remember that all life has come from God, that life must be lived and used according to His Will, that sooner or later our life must go back to God. If we use the words: "Into Thy hands I commend my spirit" in the right way, we are saying all these things to Almighty God. And if it should happen that we never wake from our sleep, then our last words, or among our very last words, will have been the same as the words that Christ used on the Cross. We could hardly find more fitting words to be our last.

After Holy Communion

The second time we should use the words: "Into Thy hands I commend my spirit" is after receiving Holy Communion. At this time we address these words to Our Lord present within us. They will then have the meaning of perfect resignation to the will of God in directing our life on earth. They will at this time also have a further special meaning, the giving of self to be remade in the image of Christ.

We are giving over the direction and the formation of our soul, "our spirit," to Christ Himself. The ultimate reason for receiving Holy Communion is to become more and more like Christ, to have Him formed in us. (*Gal.* 4:19).

This formation goes on essentially because of the growth in Sanctifying Grace, that Godlike quality that makes us adopted sons of God. Likewise, our mind, our way of thinking, of looking at things, ought to become more and more like that of Christ. As St. Paul wrote to the Philippians: "For let this mind be in you, which was also in Christ Jesus." (*Phil*. 2:5). Our heart, too, ought to become more and more like that of our Saviour. We ought to love the same things He loved, will what He willed, be sorrowful over those things that made Him sorrowful. Therefore, when we say after Holy Communion: "Into Thy hands I commend my spirit," we mean to give over our soul to Christ, asking Him to mold it more and more in His own image. We give our soul to Him, knowing that He knows best what to do for it.

Sometimes people are too much interested in trying to acquire this or that good quality, begging Our Lord to help them not to be so inclined to anger or to impatience. It would be much better to stop worrying about oneself and simply to give one's soul over to Our Lord, leaving its direction to Him.

At the Hour of Death

The third time we should use the words: "Into Thy hands I commend my spirit" is at the final hour of life. Then we have the opportunity to offer our life to God, to accept death according to His will. It would be hard to find better words than the final words of Our Lord to express the willing acceptance of death, the willing offering of life to God. "Sacred writers consider this offering of one's own life so pleasing to God that it may be compared in merit with martyrdom."*

Perhaps it may seem like a small thing to offer one's life to God, to accept death willingly, but it is not. Cynics may say it is small, since a person cannot do anything about it anyway. But to offer one's life, even though death is inevitable, is no small thing, for it is to offer back to God the most precious natural gift He has given us. To offer a million dollars for building a church or school would be a sizable gift. A dying person's life is worth more than a million dollars. He would gladly spend this if his life were spared. The value placed upon life cannot be measured in terms of money. Thus, in offering his life to God, the dying person offers his most precious natural gift.

It Is Unjust to Deceive a Dying Person

Needless to say, people who are dying should have the opportunity of freely offering the priceless gift of their life. They should not be allowed to go blindly into eternity by not being told they are dying. To try to deceive a dying person, even a child who has the use of reason, is cruelty. It is injustice.

There are a number of reasons for saying this.

---

* Toussant-Miller, *Retreat Discourses and Meditations* (1929), p. 114.

It may be that only the knowledge of approaching death will lead a person to true contrition. Even one who seems to be close to God may have been keeping something on his conscience that only the thought of death will lead him to confess. But aside from this, a person should be given the opportunity to die as Christ did, with full acceptance of the will of God. In all things we are to be imitators of Christ; therefore, we should be imitators of Him in this too. A person should not be denied the opportunity of making this final offering of life, which is so pleasing to God.

Yet, sad to say, there exists in many people a false sort of charity and a foolish softheartedness that tries to "kid" a sick person along, even through the portals of eternity. We should, of course, be optimistic and stir up the hope of living as long as there is hope. But when the danger is grave and the balance swings to the side of approaching death, then we should let the sick person know. He should not be permitted to back into eternity, but should go forward, and with his eyes open.

Well-meaning relatives sometimes try to keep all knowledge of a grave sickness from the dying person. They may even be unwilling to ask the priest to administer the "Last Rites" (Confession, Last Anointing, Communion), fearing that these may upset the sick person. But is this not misdirected affection? Is it not sentimentality instead of mercy? Certainly death is a hard fact; to be in the proximate danger of death is not a pleasant fact. But not to hear about it is not going to prevent it. To know about it in advance may be the means of a great grace, giving the dying person the opportunity to repent or the opportunity to offer his life to God.

When a person is in an accident or overcome suddenly by some sickness, the tendency among medical people is to be too hasty with the sedative needle. The doctor or hospital attendant gives a massive sedative to quiet the patient. There is a place for sedatives, but they should not be given so soon that the patient does not at least have the chance to make an act of contrition. He may not think of this himself. If you are present, you can offer to recite the Act of Contrition, asking him to pray along silently. You do not have to shock the person. Just tell him you are going to say the Act of Contrition with him "for safety sake," or something similar.

Sooner or later each person comes to his own Good Friday. It may be that for us the major pains of life will be distributed over the years, and that our last hours will not be full of suffering. Or, it may be that our last hours will be very painful. We may ask God to make it one way or the other, if we wish; it is not wrong to express our preference to Him. Yet the best attitude is to leave the choice to God: "Thy Will be done."

Study the Cross

We will be better prepared for death the more we contemplate and appreciate the Cross of

Christ and all that it means. No schooling in college or university can explain life better; no amount of reading can make us better, more real persons than can the study of the Cross. The ultimate explanation of all the mysteries of this life is bound up in the suffering and death of Jesus Christ, who is both God and man. During our life here on earth, we should study the Cross. Then, when we come to our final hour, we may have the grace to die as did Our Saviour on His Cross, with full resignation, confidence and love, saying to our Heavenly Father: "Into Thy hands I commend my spirit."

Act of Contrition

O MY GOD, I am heartily sorry for having offended Thee, and I detest all my sins because I dread the loss of Heaven and the pains of Hell; but most of all because they offend Thee, my God, Who art all good and deserving of all my love. I firmly resolve, with the help of Thy grace, to confess my sins, to do penance, and to amend my life. Amen.

If you have enjoyed this book, consider making your next selection from among the following . . .

Prices subject to change.

Holy Eucharist—Our All. *Fr. Lukas Etlin, O.S.B.* 3.00
Glories of Divine Grace. *Fr. Scheeben* 18.00
Saint Michael and the Angels. *Approved Sources* 9.00
Dolorous Passion of Our Lord. *Anne C. Emmerich* 18.00
Our Lady of Fatima's Peace Plan from Heaven. *Booklet* 1.00
Three Ways of the Spiritual Life. *Garrigou-Lagrange.* 7.00
Mystical Evolution. 2 Vols. *Fr. Arintero, O.P.* 42.00
St. Catherine Labouré of the Mirac. Medal. *Fr. Dirvin* 16.50
Manual of Practical Devotion to St. Joseph. *Patrignani.* 17.50
The Active Catholic. *Fr. Palau* 9.00
Ven. Jacinta Marto of Fatima. *Cirrincione* 3.00
Reign of Christ the King. *Davies* 2.00
St. Teresa of Avila. *William Thomas Walsh* 24.00
Isabella of Spain—The Last Crusader. *Wm. T. Walsh* 24.00
Characters of the Inquisition. *Wm. T. Walsh* 16.50
Blood-Drenched Altars—Cath. Comment. Hist. Mexico 21.50
Self-Abandonment to Divine Providence. *de Caussade.* 22.50
Way of the Cross. *Liguorian.* 1.50
Way of the Cross. *Franciscan.* 1.50
Modern Saints—Their Lives & Faces, Bk. 1. *Ann Ball* 21.00
Modern Saints—Their Lives & Faces, Bk. 2. *Ann Ball* 23.00
Divine Favors Granted to St. Joseph. *Pere Binet* 7.50
St. Joseph Cafasso—Priest of the Gallows. *St. J. Bosco* 6.00
Catechism of the Council of Trent. *McHugh/Callan* 27.50
Why Squander Illness? *Frs. Rumble & Carty* 4.00
Fatima—The Great Sign. *Francis Johnston.* 12.00
Heliotropium—Conformity of Human Will to Divine 15.00
Charity for the Suffering Souls. *Fr. John Nageleisen.* 18.00
Devotion to the Sacred Heart of Jesus. *Verheylezoon* 16.50
Sermons on Prayer. *St. Francis de Sales* 7.00
Sermons on Our Lady. *St. Francis de Sales.* 15.00
Sermons for Lent. *St. Francis de Sales* 15.00
Fundamentals of Catholic Dogma. *Ott* 27.50
Litany of the Blessed Virgin Mary. (100 cards) 5.00
Who Is Padre Pio? *Radio Replies Press* 3.00
Child's Bible History. *Knecht* 7.00
St. Anthony—The Wonder Worker of Padua. *Stoddard* 7.00
The Precious Blood. *Fr. Faber* 16.50
The Holy Shroud & Four Visions. *Fr. O'Connell* 3.50
Clean Love in Courtship. *Fr. Lawrence Lovasik* 4.50
The Secret of the Rosary. *St. Louis De Montfort* 5.00

At your Bookdealer or direct from the Publisher.
Toll-Free 1-800-437-5876   *Fax 815-226-7770*

Prices subject to change.

**Fr. Christopher
Rengers, O.F.M. Cap.**

BORN in Pittsburgh in 1917, Fr. Christopher received his elementary education at parochial schools in Pittsburgh and then attended Capuchin seminaries for high school and theology. He entered the Capuchin novitiate in Cumberland, Maryland in 1936, made his first vows in 1937 and final vows in 1940. He was ordained in Washington, D.C. on May 28, 1942. He obtained an M.A. in history from St. Louis University, taught four years, then served as a chaplain and did parish work for over 50 years on various assignments in Kansas, Missouri, Ohio, Maryland and Washington, D.C.

Fr. Christopher's writings include books entitled *The 33 Doctors of the Church*, *The Youngest Prophet* (on Jacinta Marto), *Mary of the Americas*, *The Seven Last Words* and *Saints and Sinners of Calvary*, as well as magazine articles in *Our Sunday Visitor*, *Soul*, *Priest*, *Pastoral Life*, *Homiletic and Pastoral Review*, and *Extension*.

Since 1970 Fr. Christopher has been active in the St. Joseph Medal Apostolate and its related group for the laity, The Workers of St. Joseph, both of which he founded. This work includes fostering devotion through a medal of St. Joseph and its literature, making available materials on Our Lady of Guadalupe and arranging retreat-pilgrimages to her shrine in Mexico City.

Fr. Christopher is stationed at St. Francis Friary (Capuchin College) in Washington, D.C. His current apostolates include ministering to nursing home residents and helping with hearing Confessions at the nearby National Shrine of the Immaculate Conception.